TOM BRADY, SAM CUNNINGHAM, STANLEY MORGAN, IRVING FRYAR, ROB GRONKOWSKI, VINCE WILFORK, RANDY MOSS, JULIAN EDELMAN, WES WELKER, RODNEY HARRISON, DONT'A HIGHTOWER, BEN COATES, BRUCE ARMSTRONG, TOM NEVILLE, SAM ADAMS, JON MORRIS, JULIUS ADAMS, JIM NANCE, JOHN HANNAH, RICHARD SEYMOUR, HOUSTON ANTWINE, JIM LEE HUNT, WILLIE MCGINEST, ANDRE TIPPETT, NICK BUONICONTI, TY LAW, MICHAEL HAYNES, LAWYER MILLOY, FRED MARION, ADAM VINATIERI

THE STORY OF THE NEW ENGLAND PATRIOTS

D1406764

THE STORY OF THE
NEW ENGLAND
PATRIOTS

BY JIM WHITING

CREATIVE EDUCATION / CREATIVE PAPERBACKS

PUBLISHED BY CREATIVE EDUCATION AND CREATIVE PAPERBACKS
P.O. BOX 227, MANKATO, MINNESOTA 56002
CREATIVE EDUCATION AND CREATIVE PAPERBACKS ARE IMPRINTS OF THE
CREATIVE COMPANY
WWW.THECREATIVECOMPANY.US

DESIGN AND PRODUCTION BY BLUE DESIGN (WWW.BLUEDES.COM)
ART DIRECTION BY RITA MARSHALL
PRINTED IN CHINA

PHOTOGRAPHS BY AP IMAGES (ASSOCIATED PRESS), GETTY IMAGES (ARTHUR
ANDERSON/NFL, TIMOTHY A. CLARY/AFP, SCOTT CUNNINGHAM, GIN ELLIS/
NFL PHOTOS, ELSA, FOCUS ON SPORT, OTTO GREULE JR., SCOTT HALLERAN,
WALTER IOOSS JR./SI, NICK LAHAM, STREETER LECKA, NEIL LEIFER/SI, JIM
MCISAAC, DONALD MIRALLE, RONALD C. MODRA/SPORTS IMAGERY, NFL, DOUG
PENSINGER, JOE ROBBINS, HERB SCHARFMAN/SPORTS IMAGERY, RICK STEWART
/STRINGER, JARED WICKERHAM), NEWSCOM (ABACA PRESS/HAHN LIONEL/
ABACA/SIPA USA, KEVIN DIETSCH/UPI, LESLIE PLAZA JOHNSON/ICON SPORTS-
WIRE/DBA)

COPYRIGHT © 2020 CREATIVE EDUCATION, CREATIVE PAPERBACKS
INTERNATIONAL COPYRIGHT RESERVED IN ALL COUNTRIES. NO PART OF THIS
BOOK MAY BE REPRODUCED IN ANY FORM WITHOUT WRITTEN PERMISSION
FROM THE PUBLISHER.

NAMES: WHITING, JIM, AUTHOR.
TITLE: THE STORY OF THE NEW ENGLAND PATRIOTS / JIM WHITING.
SERIES: NFL TODAY.
INCLUDES INDEX.
SUMMARY: THIS HIGH-INTEREST HISTORY OF THE NATIONAL FOOTBALL
LEAGUE'S NEW ENGLAND PATRIOTS HIGHLIGHTS MEMORABLE GAMES,
SUMMARIZES SEASONAL TRIUMPHS AND DEFEATS, AND FEATURES STANDOUT
PLAYERS SUCH AS TOM BRADY.
IDENTIFIERS: LCCN 2018059133 / ISBN 978-1-64026-150-1 (HARDCOVER) / ISBN
978-1-62832-713-7 (PBK) / ISBN 978-1-64000-268-5 (EBOOK)
SUBJECTS: LCSH: NEW ENGLAND PATRIOTS (FOOTBALL TEAM)—HISTORY—
JUVENILE LITERATURE. / NEW ENGLAND PATRIOTS (FOOTBALL TEAM)—
HISTORY.
CLASSIFICATION: LCC GV956.N36 W45 2019 / DDC 796.332/640974461—DC23

FIRST EDITION HC 9 8 7 6 5 4 3 2 1
FIRST EDITION PBK 9 8 7 6 5 4 3 2 1

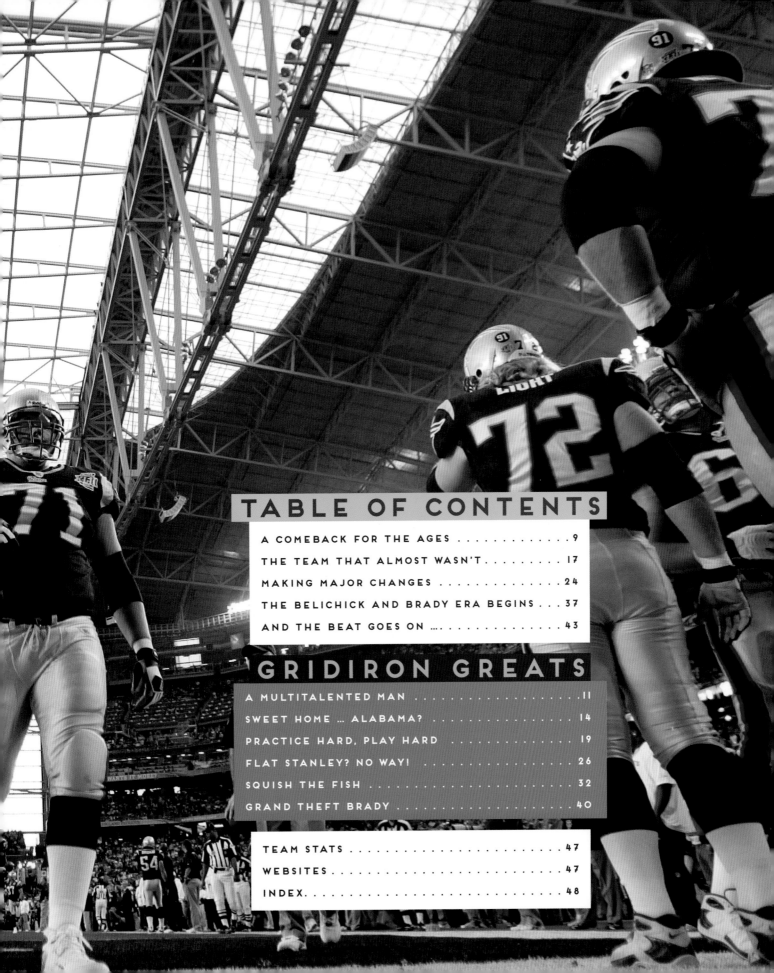

TABLE OF CONTENTS

GRIDIRON GREATS

A COMEBACK FOR THE AGES

The New England Patriots faced off against the Atlanta Falcons in Super Bowl LI. The first quarter finished with no score. Then, Atlanta's string of scoring began. The Falcons scored three touchdowns during the second quarter. At halftime, the score was 21–3. "We went into the locker room at halftime. We said the game wasn't over," said Patriots running back James White. During the third quarter, it appeared that White was wrong. Atlanta scored again. Many people thought the game was done. In the National Football League (NFL), teams rarely come back from such a lopsided margin. But with Tom Brady at quarterback, no lead is safe. He connected with White for a five-yard touchdown. But the extra point clanked off the upright.

NEW ENGLAND PATRIOTS

With less than 10 minutes remaining, Stephen Gostkowski kicked a 33-yard field goal. Then Brady threw to Danny Amendola for a touchdown. White ran a two-point conversion. That made the score 28–20. New England got the ball to its own nine-yard line. Three and a half minutes were left. Brady led the Patriots downfield again. Then receiver Julian Edelman made a key play. He caught a 23-yard pass in the midst of several defenders. He outwrestled them for the ball and kept it off the turf. White scored with one minute remaining. That narrowed the score to 28–26. Brady passed to Amendola for two more points. The game was tied. It was the first Super Bowl to go into overtime.

GRIDIRON GREATS ∨
A MULTITALENTED MAN

Gino Cappelletti played quarterback in college. But he was not drafted. He played touch football for several years. Then, he got the chance to try out for the Boston Patriots. His arm was not strong enough for professional football. He knew he would not make it as a quarterback. But he had a strong leg. He figured the team would not sign a player to just kick. So he earned a roster spot as a cornerback. In 1961, Cappelletti filled in at wide receiver. He never went back to defense. He finished his career with 1,130 points. He is third on the team's all-time scoring list.

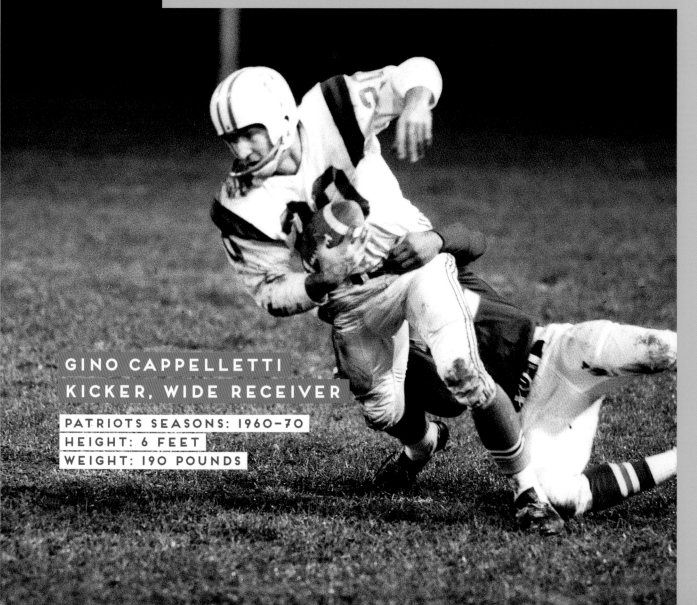

GINO CAPPELLETTI
KICKER, WIDE RECEIVER

PATRIOTS SEASONS: 1960-70
HEIGHT: 6 FEET
WEIGHT: 190 POUNDS

LINEBACKER DONT'A HIGHTOWER

"WE ALL BROUGHT EACH OTHER BACK. WE NEVER FELT OUT OF IT. IT WAS A TOUGH BATTLE. WE JUST MADE A FEW MORE PLAYS THAN THEM."

—TOM BRADY

The Patriots took the kickoff and easily moved downfield. White barreled into the end zone. The Patriots won, 34–28. "We all brought each other back. We never felt out of it. It was a tough battle.... We just made a few more plays than them," Brady said. Many people have called it the greatest Super Bowl ever. Multiple records were set or tied. It was New England's fifth Super Bowl win. All of their previous wins had been very close. This six-point margin was their largest ever. And they did not take the lead until the final play!

GRIDIRON GREATS v

SWEET HOME...ALABAMA?

In the 1960s, the Patriots played home games at Fenway Park. But the Red Sox baseball team played there, too. That meant the Patriots often started their season with several road games. Owner Billy Sullivan considered moving the team. In 1968, he set up a "home" game in Birmingham, Alabama. The Patriots played the New York Jets. Joe Namath was quarterback for the Jets. He had been a star at the University of Alabama. Most of the 30,000 fans rooted for the "visitors." It was more than twice the usual Boston-area turnout. Still, Birmingham's Legion Field was only one-third full. That was not enough for Sullivan. The Patriots stayed in Boston.

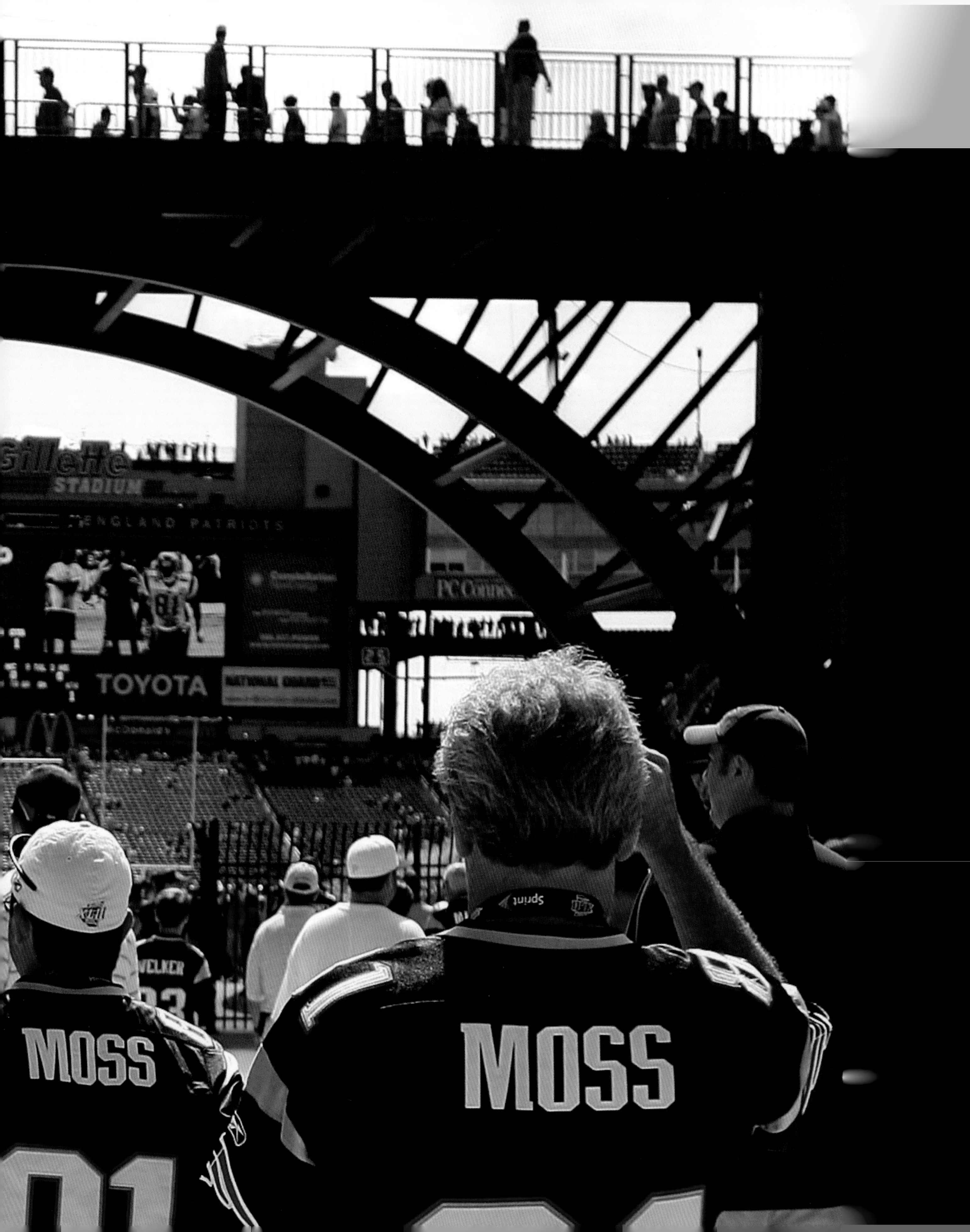
Gillette
STADIUM
TOYOTA
WELKER
MOSS
MOSS

THE TEAM THAT ALMOST WASN'T

T he New England Patriots could be called the "Team That Almost Wasn't." Boston businessman Billy Sullivan wanted to own a football team. He applied to join the upstart American Football League (AFL) in 1959. It was a rival to the National Football League (NFL). Sullivan had little money and no home stadium. But he did have a gift for persuasion. And the AFL needed an eighth team. At the time, Boston was the most populous city in the country without a professional football team. Boston

9 PRO BOWL SELECTIONS

183 GAMES PLAYED

1983

9

JOHN "HOG" HANNAH
GUARD

PATRIOTS SEASONS: 1973–85
HEIGHT: 6-FOOT-2
WEIGHT: 265 POUNDS

GRIDIRON GREATS
PRACTICE HARD, PLAY HARD

John "Hog" Hannah was one of the best offensive linemen in NFL history. Hannah seemed to underestimate himself. "I'm not a natural athlete," he said. "If I don't practice well, I won't play well." Hannah was known for practicing at full-steam all the time. In games, he exploded off the line of scrimmage. His blocks were ferocious. "He'd be responsible for blocking a linebacker on a certain play, and before you knew it, the linebacker would be down, and without slowing down, John would be out ahead taking out a cornerback," said quarterback Steve Grogan.

NEW ENGLAND PATRIOTS

19

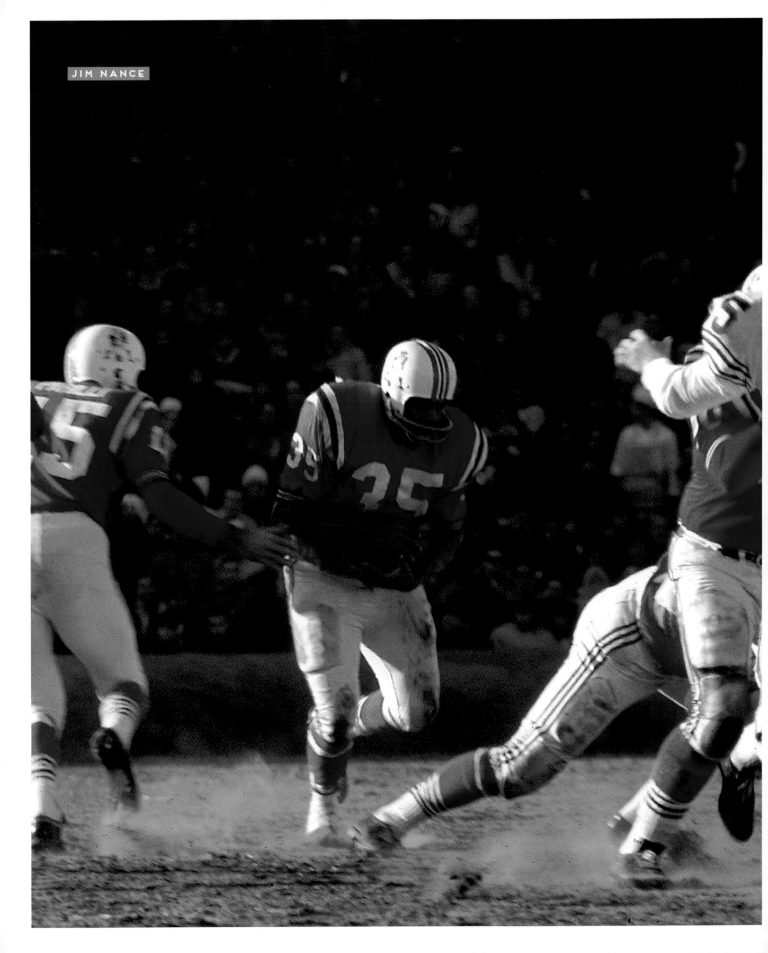

JIM NANCE

had played a key role in the Revolutionary War era. "Patriots" seemed a fitting name for the new team. More than 350 players tried out. An early standout was Gino Cappelletti. He was a key wide receiver and kicker.

Other professional teams had a home field. The Patriots did not. In its early years, the team played home games in a variety of places each year. These included Nickerson Field, Alumni Field, and Harvard Stadium. It also played several seasons at the Boston Red Sox's Fenway Park. In 1960, the Patriots finished with a 5–9 record. They improved to 9–4–1 the following season. The Patriots held steady in 1962. Then they dropped to 7–6–1 in 1963. Surprisingly, that record earned them their first postseason appearance. The Patriots tied their divisional rival, the Buffalo Bills. Boston defeated Buffalo in a playoff game. But the San Diego Chargers beat Boston, 51–10, in the AFL Championship Game.

Boston finished 1964 with 10 wins. But it missed the playoffs. The team had lackluster results for the rest of the decade. Still, players such as bulldozing fullback Jim Nance kept things exciting. In 1970, the AFL merged with the NFL. The Patriots faced new challenges. The team still had no permanent home stadium. But the NFL wanted it to have one. Various proposals in Boston failed. Finally, a plan to build a stadium in nearby Foxboro succeeded. However, the team would not based in Boston anymore. So it was renamed the New England Patriots. Unfortunately, the change of scenery didn't help. The team continued losing.

DEFENSEMEN LARRY EISENHAUER, BILLY NEIGHBORS, NICK BUONICONTI, RON HALL, AND GINO CAPPELLETTI

"THE '76 TEAM WAS THE BEST I EVER PLAYED ON."

—JOHN "HOG" HANNAH

In 1976, the Patriots finally found success. They won 11 games. Key players were offensive lineman John "Hog" Hannah and tight end Russ Francis. Cornerback Mike Haynes was Defensive Rookie of the Year. The Patriots earned their first postseason berth in 13 years. "The '76 team was the best I ever played on," Hannah said. That talented Patriots team met the Oakland Raiders in the first round of playoffs. The game became notorious. Fans thought the officials made numerous questionable calls. One New England offensive lineman who had gone the entire season without a holding penalty was flagged three times for holding. Oakland came back from a 21–10 deficit. It scored a touchdown with 10 seconds left. The Raiders won, 24–21.

QUARTERBACK JIM PLUNKETT

MAKING MAJOR CHANGES

RUNNING BACKS ANDY JOHNSON (LEFT) AND SAM CUNNINGHAM

ew England came back strong in 1978. It enjoyed an 11–5 record. Rookie wide receiver Stanley Morgan showed glimpses of his immense talent. For the first time, the Patriots had home-field advantage in the playoffs. But the Houston Oilers pummeled them, 31–14. During the next six years, the Patriots had just one postseason appearance.

In 1985, New England started at 2–3. But it rallied to finish 11–5. Running back Craig James piled up more than 1,500 total yards. In the

GRIDIRON GREATS v

FLAT STANLEY? NO WAY!

Stanley Morgan, wrote one reporter, was a "touchdown waiting to happen." He averaged 19.4 yards per reception in an era when defensive backs were permitted to bang receivers all the way down the field. Once he caught the ball, Morgan was a speeding bullet. Often, he was gone before defenders could get a hand on him. "I remember Stanley going deep on those go-routes with nobody around to catch him," said linebacker Andre Tippett. "Whenever you saw him open like that, you knew it was going to be a touchdown." His 10,352 receiving yards are the most in team history.

72

72 CAREER RECEIVING TOUCHDOWNS

196

196 GAMES PLAYED

playoffs, New England won three games on the road. The team headed to its first Super Bowl. There, the Chicago Bears crushed the Patriots, 46–10. The Patriots had found success through the running game during the regular season. But in the Super Bowl, they came out passing. The change might have been a factor in the defeat. "Well, the one thing the Bears can't say today is they stopped our running game," said James. "Because we didn't run it."

New England went 11–5 again in 1986. In the postseason, it lost to the Denver Broncos. After that, the team missed the playoffs for seven years. It hit rock bottom in 1990. The Patriots managed just one win. Despite the dismal record, their final home game was sold out. They faced the New York Giants. Giants fans filled the stadium. Home games in New York were always sellouts. So thousands of New Yorkers trooped north to Boston. Tickets were readily available.

ANDRE TIPPETT

Two years later, Patriots won just two games. They knew they had to make big changes. First, the team hired Bill Parcells as coach. He had won two Super Bowls with the Giants. Then the Patriots focused on the quarterback position. They selected Drew Bledsoe with the first overall pick of the 1993 NFL Draft. In his second year, Bledsoe led New England to its first playoff appearance since 1986.

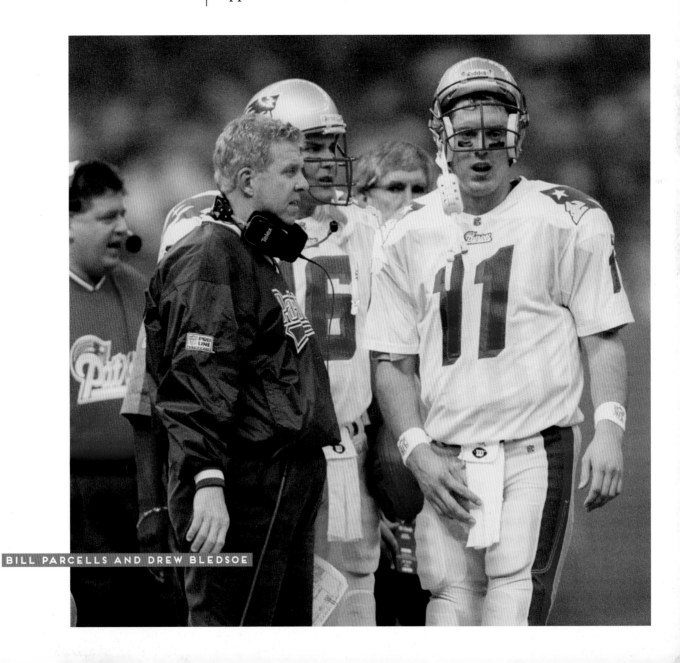

BILL PARCELLS AND DREW BLEDSOE

GRIDIRON GREATS ∨
SQUISH THE FISH

The Patriots played the Miami Dolphins for the 1985 conference championship. History was not on their side. They had not won a game in Miami's Orange Bowl stadium since 1966. But the Patriots took advantage of soggy field conditions. "'Oh, boy,' we thought, 'we're gonna run the ball in the mud,'" said center Pete Brock. "And we did." The Patriots rushed for 255 yards. They also recovered four Miami fumbles. The game concluded in a 31–14 New England victory. "It was 'Squish the Fish,'" said linebacker Andre Tippett. "We weren't going to be denied."

**AFC CHAMPIONSHIP GAME
PATRIOTS VS. MIAMI DOLPHINS**

ORANGE BOWL
MIAMI, FLORIDA
JANUARY 12, 1986

6

6 TURNOVERS RECOVERED BY PATRIOTS

255

255 RUSHING YARDS (PATRIOTS)

The 10–6 Patriots took on the 11–5 Cleveland Browns in the Wild Card. New England lost. Two years later, the Patriots went 11–5. They trounced the Pittsburgh Steelers in a foggy playoff game. Then they dispatched the Jacksonville Jaguars in a chilly American Football Conference (AFC) Championship Game. In Super Bowl XXXI, they faced the Green Bay Packers. By halftime, the Patriots had fallen behind. They could not get back in the game. The Packers won, 35–21. Parcells left the team after the defeat. His successor was Pete Carroll. He lasted just three years. Owner Robert Kraft fired him. Once again, it was time for a change.

BILL BELICHICK

THE BELICHICK AND BRADY ERA BEGINS

The Patriots made two brilliant moves in 2000. One was hiring Bill Belichick as coach. The other was drafting quarterback Tom Brady. The brilliance wasn't immediately obvious. Many fans thought Belichick's hiring had been a mistake. He had compiled a losing record during his five-year stint as the Browns' head coach. New England finished 5–11 in Belichick's first season. The poor record seemed to prove the doubters correct. As for Brady, few people paid any attention. He played in just one game that season. Two of his three passes were incomplete.

Belichick had a plan. He wanted to assemble a group of team players. Together, they would achieve more than individual stars. This plan began to fall into place in 2001. Near the end of the second regular-season game, Bledsoe was injured. Brady stepped in. The Patriots lost. For the next eight games, Brady's play was spotty. Still, Belichick saw something in the young

WIDE RECEIVER WES WELKER

quarterback. It wasn't pure physical ability. Brady was a natural leader.

Bledsoe recovered. But Belichick stuck with Brady. The coach's faith in him paid off. The Patriots won their last six games of the regular season. After two playoff wins, New England rolled into Super Bowl XXXVI. It faced the heavily favored St. Louis Rams. The Patriots shocked the Rams. They won, 20–17, on a last-second field goal by kicker Adam Vinatieri. "You can't beat a team like the Rams with individuals," said safety Lawyer Milloy. "It takes a team. That's what you saw today."

New England fell to 9–7 in 2002. But teamwork and smart play kept the team on track. In 2003, it won 14 games. It tore through the playoffs. The Patriots met the Carolina Panthers in Super Bowl XXXVIII. The game came down to the wire. In the fourth quarter, the score was tied at 29. Brady led his team down the field. Once again, Vinatieri sealed the victory. He kicked a 41-yard field goal with nine seconds remaining. New England won, 32–29. The next year, the Patriots went 14–2 again. They plowed through the playoffs. In the Super Bowl, they took on the Philadelphia Eagles. The Patriots' defense held off a late Eagles charge. New England won its third Super Bowl, 24–21.

The Patriots had good seasons in 2005 and 2006. But they lost in the playoffs. Then, in 2007, New England came close to football immortality. The team went undefeated in the regular season. It scored 589 points. That was an NFL record. The Patriots beat the Jaguars and the Chargers in the playoffs. New England reached its fourth Super Bowl in seven years. It stood poised to become the first 19–0 team in NFL history. The heavily favored Patriots met the Giants in Super Bowl XLII. New England led with less than three minutes remaining. But a late drive carried the Giants downfield. New York scored a touchdown with 39 seconds left. The Patriots were disappointed as the Giants won, 17–14. "I think we all feel the same way," Belichick said. "I wish we could have done one thing a little better, and it might have changed it. But we didn't."

WIDE RECEIVER RANDY MOSS

GRIDIRON GREATS v
GRAND THEFT BRADY

Tom Brady began his career at the University of Michigan. He became the starter as a junior. He performed well as the starter. But NFL teams paid little attention to him. He was one of the slowest quarterbacks at the 2000 NFL Combine. Despite that, the Patriots liked his quick thinking and leadership skills. But they already had three quarterbacks. They finally picked Brady in the sixth round of the Draft. Brady took over when the starting quarterback was injured in 2001. Since then, he has piled up many achievements. Brady is sometimes called the greatest steal in NFL Draft history.

TOM BRADY
QUARTERBACK

PATRIOTS SEASONS: 2000-PRESENT
HEIGHT: 6-FOOT-4
WEIGHT: 225 POUNDS

NEW ENGLAND PATRIOTS

41

AND THE BEAT GOES ON ...

I n 2008, Brady suffered a knee injury early in the first game. New England's title hopes went down with him. He was out for the entire year. Brady returned in 2009. He earned Comeback Player of the Year honors. The Patriots advanced to the postseason. But the Baltimore Ravens glided to a 33–14 triumph in the Wild Card game. The following year, Brady had another impressive season. He earned the league's MVP award. The Patriots topped the AFC. But the New York Jets eliminated them in the first round of the playoffs.

In 2011, New England went 13–3. Tight end Rob Gronkowski helped fuel the winning record. He had quickly become one of Brady's favorite

NEW ENGLAND PATRIOTS

43

targets. The 6-foot-6 and 265-pound "Gronk" scored 18 touchdowns in 2011. He also had 1,327 receiving yards. Those were NFL records for tight ends. Bledsoe summed up the matchup problems Gronkowski created. "It's kind of like having [basketball star] LeBron James playing tight end for you," he said. "He's too big for the slow guys and too fast for the small guys." Unfortunately, Gronkowski suffered a severe ankle sprain in the AFC title game. This limited his playing ability in Super Bowl XLVI. The Giants foiled the Patriots. They pulled out a 21–17 victory.

The Patriots compiled 12–4 marks in the following two seasons. Both times, they lost in the conference championship game. In 2014, they finished at 12–4 for the third year in a row. This time, they advanced to the Super Bowl. They faced the Seattle Seahawks. The Patriots trailed 24–14 in the fourth quarter. Then they scored twice to take the lead. But the Seahawks flew downfield. Seattle had the ball on the one-yard line. Just 26 seconds remained. Rather than hand the ball to bruising running back Marshawn Lynch, the Seahawks called a pass play. Rookie cornerback Malcolm Butler became an instant hero for New England. He burst in front of the intended receiver and intercepted the ball. The Patriots won.

In the 2015 AFC Championship Game, New England faced the Broncos. New England had the NFL's top offense. Denver boasted the league's best defense. The Broncos had the best of the exchange. The Patriots scored a touchdown with mere seconds left. The score was narrowed to 18–16. But Brady's attempted pass for a tying

MALCOLM BUTLER

ROB GRONKOWSKI

CORNERBACK STEPHON GILMORE

two-point conversion was intercepted.

New England captured its fifth Super Bowl title in 2016. It beat the Falcons in overtime. The following year, the Patriots made their eighth Super Bowl appearance in 17 years. Despite the Patriots being favored to win, the high-scoring game ended with the Eagles prevailing, 41–33. The following year, the Patriots redeemed themselves in Super Bowl LIII with a 13–3 win over the Los Angeles Rams.

Since the beginning of the 21st century, the Patriots have racked up impressive regular-season records. The franchise has also captured numerous Super Bowl victories. Other contenders go through cycles of boom and bust. Lately, the Patriots have shown a knack for finding talent. This has kept them consistently at the top of the standings. With a combination of crafty coaching, tight-knit team play, and their trademark tenacity, the Patriots seem poised to fulfill their Super Bowl dreams yet again.

NFL CHAMPIONSHIPS

2001, 2003, 2004, 2014, 2016, 2018

WEBSITES

NEW ENGLAND PATRIOTS

https://www.patriots.com/

NFL: NEW ENGLAND PATRIOTS TEAM PAGE

http://www.nfl.com/teams/newenglandpatriots/profile?team=NE

NEW ENGLAND PATRIOTS

INDEX

2008 NEW ENGLAND DEFENSE